NP

DEC   2023

Question, connect and take action to become better citizens with a brighter future. Now that's smart thinking!

BREAKING NEWS
WHY MEDIA MATTERS

RAINA DELISLE

illustrated by Julie McLaughlin

ORCA BOOK PUBLISHERS

Published in Canada and the United States in 2023 by Orca Book Publishers.
orcabook.com

Library and Archives Canada Cataloguing in Publication

Title: Breaking news : why media matters / Raina Delisle ; illustrated by Julie McLaughlin.
Names: Delisle, Raina, author. | McLaughlin, Julie, 1984- illustrator.
Series: Orca think ; 10.
Description: Series statement: Orca think ; 10 | Includes bibliographical references and index.
Identifiers: Canadiana (print) 20220266018 | Canadiana (ebook) 20220266026 |
ISBN 9781459826564 (hardcover) | ISBN 9781459826571 (PDF) | ISBN 9781459826588 (EPUB)
Subjects: LCSH: Press—Juvenile literature. | LCSH: Journalism—Juvenile literature. |
LCSH: Journalism—Social aspects—Juvenile literature.
Classification: LCC PN4731 .D44 2023 | DDC j070.4—dc23

Library of Congress Control Number: 2022939918

Summary: Part of the nonfiction Orca Think series for middle-grade readers, this
illustrated book introduces kids to the news media and why it matters.

Orca Book Publishers is committed to reducing the consumption of nonrenewable resources in the
production of our books. We make every effort to use materials that support a sustainable future.

Orca Book Publishers gratefully acknowledges the support for its publishing programs provided
by the following agencies: the Government of Canada, the Canada Council for the Arts and the
Province of British Columbia through the BC Arts Council and the Book Publishing Tax Credit.

Supported by the Province of British Columbia

Cover and interior artwork by Julie McLaughlin
Design by Troy Cunningham
Edited by Kirstie Hudson

Printed and bound in South Korea.

26 25 24 23 • 1 2 3 4

This book is dedicated to all the young journalists
from marginalized communities who are working
hard to improve the media industry.

Contents

Introduction

When I was in elementary school, I landed my first job in journalism as a newspaper carrier. Twice a week stacks of newspapers arrived on my doorstep, hot off the press. (Sometimes the papers were actually still warm!) I usually read the paper cover to cover before starting my delivery route. I was a curious kid and loved being one of the first people to know what was happening in my community. My curiosity grew as I got older. I started reading my mom's magazines and watching the evening news on television. In high school I took a journalism class and was hooked.

At university I volunteered for the student newspaper and became editor in chief in my final year. I saw firsthand the many important roles the paper played. It let people know what was happening in the community and the wider world. It celebrated people's successes and highlighted their challenges. It made sure powerful people were keeping their promises and taking responsibility when they made mistakes.

When I was a kid, I was featured in my local newspaper a few times. Once I was even asked for my opinion on provincial politics!
RAINA DELISLE

1

My older daughter followed in my footsteps and got a paper route when she was eight. Here, my younger daughter and I give her a hand.
GABRIEL GOERS

The St Bride Library, where I worked for a couple of years, opened way back in 1895 and is home to the biggest collection of type in the world.
COURTESY OF ST BRIDE LIBRARY

And it provided readers with the information they needed to make important decisions in their lives. Back then social media didn't exist, so reading the paper was a big part of how people stayed informed and connected.

I moved to London, England, after I graduated and started working at the St Bride Library, one of the most famous printing libraries in the world. I was surrounded by old newspapers, printing presses and thousands of metal rectangles with raised letters on them, kind of like stamps. These letters, called type, used to be laid out one by one to form words and stories in newspapers hundreds of years ago. Just imagine how much work that was! Naturally, I became fascinated by the history of the media industry.

I returned to Canada a couple of years later and started working in the news business. I've been a reporter, editor and producer for newspapers, magazines, television news shows and online publications

Today you can easily change the font on your computer, but in the past typographers had to create new sets of type to make words in different styles.
FERRANTRAITE/GETTY IMAGES

across Canada. In 2022 I started working in government communications, giving me a new perspective on the media industry. I still occasionally write stories for my favorite publications.

The media industry has changed a lot since I got my first job as a professional journalist in 2005, largely due to the growth of the internet and social media. In North America thousands of newspapers have closed, tens of thousands of journalists have lost their jobs and trust in the media has dropped to an all-time low. At the same time, fake and misleading news has been on the rise right when we need accurate and reliable information more than ever to understand major world events like the COVID-19 pandemic and climate change. The good news is new models of journalism are emerging, new technologies are changing the way news is created and consumed, and journalists are working hard to improve the public's trust in their work.

Grab a notebook and join me as I take you behind the headlines and show you how the news is made, what influence it has on our lives, what it may look like in the future and how you can be a part of it.

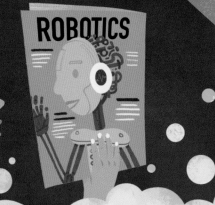

ONE
News You Can Use

THE WRITING ON THE WALL

What's new? It's one of the most common questions we ask one another. People have always wanted to know the latest news because they're curious, they enjoy talking about it and they want to get the information they need to live their best lives. You can't vote in an election, go to a community gathering or prepare for a snowstorm if you don't know they're happening!

Long before there were newspapers, radios, televisions and the internet— and even before writing was invented— people were sharing news by painting and carving messages on and into rocks.

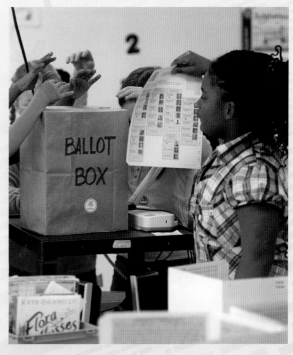

If you follow the news, you'll never miss out on important events like elections. YMCA CENTER FOR YOUTH VOICE

The Altamira cave in Spain is famous for its prehistoric pictographs and petroglyphs, including these paintings of horses. In 1879 Marcelino Sanz de Sautuola was exploring the cave with his eight-year-old daughter, Maria, when she pointed out paintings of bison on the ceiling, kicking off a major discovery.

JESUS DE FUENSANTA/SHUTTERSTOCK.COM

Pictographs and **petroglyphs** date back tens of thousands of years and can be found all over the world. Early humans used red *ochre*, natural dyes and stone tools to create pictures and symbols. They etched and sketched people, animals, shapes and lines. No one knows for sure what it all meant or why they did this, but some researchers think it was to communicate important messages, kind of like prehistoric newspapers.

REED "PENCILS" AND CLAY "PAPER"

Some historians think people first invented writing roughly 5,500 years ago in Mesopotamia, in what is now Iraq. People used reeds to make "pencils" and wrote on clay "paper" in wedge-shaped "letters." This form of writing became known as *cuneiform*, which means "wedge-shaped."

Some experts think cuneiform was invented to keep track of **rations** of beer and bread. They also think it was used to record other information, like board-game instructions, spells to keep demons away and the news of the day. Eventually people figured out how to make paper out of plants and animal skins, and ink out of burnt wood and oil, making it a whole lot easier to share the news. Imagine a whole newspaper made out of clay tablets!

Cuneiform tablets were baked in the sun or a kiln. Some of them could fit in the palm of your hand, just like an iPhone.

THE ORIGINAL NEWSCASTERS

One effective way to share the news is to find the loudest person around and get them to belt it out at the top of their lungs, which is exactly what many of the first communities in the world did. These original newscasters became known as *town criers*.

One of the first town criers may have been the ancient Greek warrior Stentor. According to Greek mythology, he was responsible for delivering news to the Greek army during the Trojan War and had a voice as loud as 50 men.

He even inspired a new word, *stentor*, which means "a person with a loud voice."

Town criers were particularly popular in medieval England. Back then most people couldn't read or write, so they relied on town criers to get the scoop on everything from wars and plagues to royal births and deaths by execution.

These early broadcasters often stood in town squares, rang bells and called out, "Oyez, oyez, oyez!" (pronounced "oh yay") to get everyone's attention. They would then read the news from a scroll and post it outside a public building for all to see. Town criers and the practice of posting the news inspired many newspaper owners to name their publications the *Crier* or the *Post*.

As more and more people learned to read and write, and as newspapers started circulating, town criers started hanging up their bells. Today some communities still have town criers just for fun. There are even town crier competitions. Oyez, oyez, oyez!

DAILY EVENTS

While town criers were belting out the news, other people were quietly at work developing newspapers. Some historians think several ancient societies had handwritten newspapers. The most famous was the Roman Empire's *Acta Diurna* (daily events), which was published more than 2,000 years ago. The daily publication

Geschriebene Zeitung aus dem Jahre 1536.

covered births, deaths, accidents, crimes, festivals, legal decisions, military battles, government activities and even human-interest stories, which are stories about people that appeal to our emotions. In other words, the same stuff you see in newspapers today. However, *Acta Diurna* was controlled by the government, so it probably didn't include any news that made the empire look bad!

Scribes made copies of *Acta Diurna*, and delivery people posted them in public places and dropped them off on people's doorsteps, just like newspaper carriers today. No one knows how many copies scribes made, but imagine how tired your hand would get writing out the same thing over and over and over again!

START THE PRESSES

For centuries people around the world were developing printing presses, which are machines that quickly produce multiple copies of printed materials. At first people carved text backward into wood blocks, applied ink to the blocks and printed them on paper or fabric. Then, about a thousand years ago, a Chinese inventor named Bi Sheng came up with a better way of doing things. He carved individual characters (similar to letters) into clay, arranged them on a frame and then started printing. These characters, which became known as *moveable type*, could be reused, saving printers a ton of time and effort.

In the 1440s a German inventor named Johannes Gutenberg improved on Bi Sheng's printing press by creating movable type made out of metal, an ink that stuck to metal and transferred to paper, and a press that applied firm and even pressure to printing surfaces. The Gutenberg press and printed newspapers soon spread throughout Europe and, eventually, around the world.

In 1810 another German inventor, Friedrich Koenig, kicked printing into high gear when he figured out how to hook up a printing press to a **steam engine**. While the Gutenberg press could print about 250 sheets per hour, a steam-powered press could print quadruple that. Printing

HOE'S SIX CYLINDER PRINTING PRESS.

Several inventors created printing presses that worked in different ways. American Richard March Hoe designed this printing press, which looks like a jungle gym, in the 1860s. Printers placed the type on a rotating cylinder rather than on a flat bed, which allowed newspapers to be printed much faster.

technology continued to advance, and today some of the fastest presses can print 100,000 sheets per hour!

Together, printing presses and newspapers had a huge impact on societies. They made it possible for people to share information and ideas quickly and widely. They helped people understand what was happening in their communities and connect with one another. They inspired more people to learn how to read, creating more educated societies. And they stirred up a lot of trouble as some leaders didn't want the public knowing what they were up to.

FREEDOM OF THE PRESS

As more individuals and groups started newspapers, some powerful people became increasingly worried that publications would print ideas and information that challenged their power. As a result, some political and religious authorities

Former US first lady Eleanor Roosevelt holds the Universal Declaration of Human Rights, which says, "everyone has the right to freedom of opinion and expression; this right includes freedom to hold opinions without interference and to seek, receive and impart information and ideas through any media and regardless of frontiers."

FDR PRESIDENTIAL LIBRARY & MUSEUM/ WIKIMEDIA COMMONS/CC BY-SA 2.0

censored publications, which means they didn't allow them to publish anything they deemed unacceptable.

That started changing in 1766, when Sweden became the first country to pass a law guaranteeing freedom of the press. This law prevented the government from censoring printed material and allowed journalists to publish information about the government's activities. It also allowed everyday people to express ideas and share information without worrying about getting in trouble. Several countries followed Sweden's lead, and the United Nations included freedom of the press in the 1948 *Universal Declaration of Human Rights*. However, many governments still restrict press freedom, which you will learn more about in chapter 4.

GROWING PAINS

Have you ever had a pain in your leg and blamed it on growing too fast? Newspapers also experienced growing pains as they rapidly multiplied around the world. Here are some of the biggest issues with newspapers in the early days.

Classism

Newspapers were expensive to print and purchase, so only rich people could get the news. They became more affordable in the 1830s when publishers started using steam-powered printing presses to mass produce cheap newspapers. In the United States these papers became known as the *penny press* because they only cost a penny while other papers typically cost six cents.

Politicism

Political parties financially supported most newspapers from the 1780s to the 1830s in what became known as the *party press era*. As a result, newspapers published stories that made the parties that supported them look good and didn't publish stories that made them look bad. This started changing as the concept of press freedom caught on and the penny press became more popular. Newspapers no longer needed to rely on money from political parties because printing was so cheap and they could make money by selling more papers as well as advertisements. Readers also became more interested in newspapers that claimed to be **impartial**.

Sensationalism

To attract readers, newspapers published a lot of sensational stories that exaggerated the facts or weren't totally accurate. This became known as *yellow journalism* in the 1890s, when the *New York Journal* and the *New York World* fought to dominate the market by publishing sensational stories. The name comes from the Yellow Kid, the main character in a popular comic strip that was drawn by a cartoonist the *Journal* had hired away from the *World*. The papers published such sensational stories about Cuba's struggle for independence from Spain that some experts say they contributed to the Spanish-American war. Eventually the public became tired of fake news, the courts started to hold journalists accountable and newspapers developed codes of ethics, which are rules journalists are expected to follow.

The Yellow Kid was a comic-strip character from the late 1800s. He was drawn with a shaved head to suggest he'd recently had lice.
RICHARD FELTON OUTCAULT/WIKIMEDIA COMMONS/PUBLIC DOMAIN

Sexism

Newspapers were largely produced by and for men, so they didn't represent the views and interests of women. Some newspapers had "women's pages," which contained stories that were supposedly of interest to women. These pages typically covered the four Fs—family, food, furnishings and fashion—and were designed to appeal to upper-class women who could afford luxuries. When women were hired as journalists, they faced discrimination. They usually worked on the women's pages and had to fight to get more serious assignments. While women's pages gave women a rare opportunity to express themselves and see themselves represented in newspapers, they also reinforced stereotypes and class differences.

Racism

Newspapers typically did a poor job of telling the stories of people from racialized communities and treated them unfairly. For instance, white journalists in the United States were often racist against African Americans. These journalists portrayed Black people as dangerous and inferior, sensationalized reports of crimes they allegedly committed, ignored their concerns, supported discriminatory practices such as slavery and mocked them in cartoons.

Unfortunately, the media industry is still experiencing some of these same growing pains today.

H. J. MYERS/WIKIMEDIA COMMONS/PUBLIC DOMAIN

STAR REPORTER:
NELLIE BLY

In the early 1880s, 18-year-old Elizabeth Cochrane read an article in the *Pittsburgh Dispatch* entitled "What Girls Are Good For." The article said women should stay home and cook and clean rather than go to work. She was outraged and sent a letter to the editor. The editor was so impressed with her writing that he hired her as a reporter. Using the **pen name** Nellie Bly, she wrote about important issues like women's rights, but her editor also sometimes assigned her to the women's pages.

In search of more serious work, she headed to New York City and burst into the office of Joseph Pulitzer, owner of the *New York World*. He decided to give her a chance and a dangerous assignment—go undercover at an insane asylum. By pretending to be mentally ill, Nellie was admitted to the asylum, where she stayed for 10 days and witnessed horrific abuse. Her *exposé* shocked the public and led to a government investigation and changes at the asylum. She later convinced her editor to allow her to attempt to travel around the world faster than the main character in the fictional book *Around the World in Eighty Days*. (She did it in 72.) Nellie inspired many other women to become investigative journalists and international adventurers.

"If you want to do it, you can do it." —Nellie Bly

BEHIND THE HEADLINES

A group of Black leaders came together in New York City in 1827 to launch the first African American newspaper, *Freedom's Journal.* They established the weekly paper to counter the racist coverage in mainstream newspapers, voice their concerns and opinions, create a sense of **solidarity** among African Americans and encourage their community members to learn to read and write. "We wish to plead our own cause. Too long have others spoken for us," the editors wrote in the first issue.

Freedom's Journal covered issues that mattered to African Americans but were largely ignored by white journalists, such as crimes against them, civil rights and ending slavery. The paper also published positive stories about Black people, as well as poems, essays and speeches.

However, after only two years of publishing, the paper folded. Still, *Freedom's Journal* made a major impact. It advanced the **abolitionist** and civil rights movements, educated and empowered many Black people, and paved the way for more African Americans and people from other **marginalized** communities to publish newspapers.

A PICTURE IS WORTH A THOUSAND WORDS

Have you ever heard the expression "a picture is worth a thousand words"? It means that an image can get an idea across much faster than words. Pictures draw us into stories and help us see things for ourselves.

In the early 1800s, before photography was invented, newspapers started hiring artists to draw pictures of events to accompany stories. Some historians think the first photograph to appear in a newspaper was published by the French publication *L'Illustration* in 1848. It showed barricades that had been built by protesters in a Paris street during June Days, a civil uprising over workers' rights. Newspapers went on to occasionally print photos of wars and other major events, but it wasn't until photography equipment and technology improved around the 1920s that photos in newspapers became common. Today, choosing what photo to put on the front page of the paper is one of the biggest decisions editors make.

This 1848 photo of barricades in a Paris street may have been the first photo ever published in a newspaper.

THIBAULT/WIKIMEDIA COMMONS/ PUBLIC DOMAIN

HEAR AND NOW

On Christmas Eve in 1906, Reginald Fessenden, a Canadian inventor, made the first long-distance radio broadcast of the human voice. (He sang Christmas carols, but apparently not very well!) Newspaper owners soon began to worry that radio stations would start broadcasting the news and readers would tune in and stop buying the paper. The owners of the *Detroit News* decided to start their own news radio station to hang on to their audience. They didn't know how to build a radio station, so they hired teenage radio pioneer Michael DeLisle Lyons to do it for them. Unsure if the station would be a success or a failure, the owners also got the teen to get government permission for the station in his name so they could blame him if it was a bust.

The station, called 8MK, broadcast what some historians believe was the first radio news program in 1920. Fortunately, it was a success, and the station (now called WWJ Newsradio 950 and no longer owned by the newspaper) is still operating today.

Radio changed the news in many ways:

Three men prepare for a broadcast by 8MK in the 1920s. Back then they used a device called a phonograph to record and reproduce sound.

DETROIT NEWS/WIKIMEDIA COMMONS/ PUBLIC DOMAIN

- It allowed people to hear events and the voices of people involved in them, making for a much more emotional and exciting experience.
- It made the news more accessible to people from different classes and backgrounds. People who couldn't read could listen to the news, and people who were too busy to read the paper (like a working single mother) could tune in while they did other tasks (like making school lunches).

Before TV was invented, families would gather around the radio and listen to the news.

FPG/GETTY IMAGES

- It enabled people to get the news faster. If there was a massive accident on the highway, people could hear about it on the radio and avoid the area rather than sit in traffic for hours and read about what had happened in the newspaper the next day.

SEEING IS BELIEVING

Have you seen the movie *Up*? In the opening scene, a young Carl Fredricksen goes to the movie theater to watch a news story about an explorer's efforts to capture the beast of Paradise Falls. As far back as the early 1900s, before television was invented, people went to movie theaters to watch the news on film. These productions were called *newsreels* and were usually shown before movies.

As television sets started becoming more common in living rooms around the world in the 1940s and 1950s, several TV stations started producing daily newscasts. At first these newscasts were only about 10 or 15 minutes long, and a host would simply read the news on air, sometimes showing maps or photos. As technology advanced, TV news programs started showing prerecorded scenes from events and, later, live events.

People liked TV news so much, stations dedicated to covering news 24 hours a day started launching in the 1980s. This created what's known as the *24-hour news cycle*, which means that news is collected, updated and published around the clock.

TV changed the news in one big way: it allowed people to see news events for themselves. This made people more likely to believe the news, have an emotional reaction to it and build community around it, which in turn made them more likely to take action. For instance, researchers found that the majority of Americans who watched media coverage of the 9/11 terrorist attacks felt sad or frightened but also more patriotic and more supportive of government and military actions against the attackers.

ALASHI/GETTY IMAGES

GOING ONLINE

When you want to get the scoop on something right away—the results of an election or the status of a storm, for example—you can go online, google it and click on a news site. After the World Wide Web launched in 1993, media outlets started creating websites and publishing their stories online, changing the way news is produced and consumed.

After social media sites like Facebook and Twitter came online in the 2000s, media outlets started sharing their stories on them and people started looking to them for news.

The internet and social media have had several positive effects on the news industry and audiences:

- They've allowed media organizations to reach bigger audiences and given people the opportunity to get the news from different outlets.
- They've made it easier for people to launch new media outlets like online news sites and podcasts.
- They've allowed people to get the news whenever they want from the comfort of their homes or while they're out and about, as long as they have a device connected to the internet.
- They've enabled journalists to more easily research their stories and find sources.
- They've allowed readers to be more engaged in the news by joining online discussions on media outlets' websites and social media pages.

The internet and social media have also presented a number of challenges for the media industry, which you will learn about in chapter 4.

EXTRA! EXTRA!

Utah teenager Philo Farnsworth came up with the idea for the first electronic TV system when he was a high-school chemistry student in the 1920s and completed the prototype when he was 21. Unfortunately, RCA, an electronics company that's still around today, claimed to have the idea first, leading to a legal battle. Fortunately, one of Farnsworth's teachers had kept a drawing the student had done of his invention, helping him win the case and $1 million from RCA.

NEWS DAILY

LOCAL   NATIONAL   WORLD   TRENDING

TECH   SPORTS   CULTURE   WEATHER   OPINION

Headlines

Meteor lands in Spring Hills neighborhood, no injuries reported

LOCAL

TRENDING

Man bites dog!

OPINION

President's new pink hair a refreshing change

TECH

Have you tried turning it off and on again?

TWO
Media
Matters

How do you find out what's going on in your community, your country and the world? Do you read your local newspaper? Or do you prefer radio, television or online news? Maybe you enjoy relaxing with a magazine in the bath—my personal favorite. Or perhaps you rely on your parents, teachers, friends or random strangers on Facebook to fill you in. (I don't recommend the last one.)

If you don't follow the news yet, don't worry. Lots of people don't start paying attention until they're adults—and lots of adults don't even bother. People often avoid the news because they find it depressing, overwhelming or untrustworthy, but more on that later. Still, there are plenty of reasons to tune in. Here are a few.

Geoffery Rogers started reporting the news from his hometown of Rochester, NY, and launched a media outlet, the GSL SHOW, in 2014, when he was 12 years old. He shares his reports through his website, podcast and social media accounts.
GEOFFERY ROGERS

21

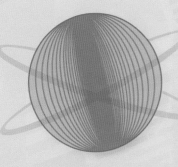

It helps you become a more informed and engaged citizen

When you know what's going on around you, you can get involved and make a difference. If you hear on the radio that your city council is planning a community meeting to discuss plans for a new playground, you can show up with your friends and share your thoughts on what you would like to see. Gaga ball pit anyone?

It opens your mind and broadens your worldview

The news can take you around the world in minutes, helping you better understand and appreciate what's happening outside your community. You can learn about everything from wars in the Middle East to famines in Africa and from animals migrating across the sea to billionaires racing to outer space.

It gives you more interesting things to talk about

Did you hear about the five-year-old who snatched the keys to his family car and drove along a highway in Utah before he was pulled over by the police? How about the raccoon that got stuck in a vending machine at a high school in Florida? And then there was Twiggy, the waterskiing squirrel, who was banned from shredding waves in Toronto. Seriously, you can't make this stuff up! If you follow the news, you'll learn something new every day and always have something interesting to talk about.

INFORMATION EXPERTS

Journalism plays many important roles. Its primary purpose is to give us the information we need to help us make the best decisions about our lives, our communities and our governments.

Journalists gather information about issues, events and people and then put together stories and share them with the public. They have to spend a lot of time asking people questions, digging for information and verifying that everything is accurate, using techniques they learned in school or on the job. Most people don't have the time, skills or interest to do this themselves. Journalists provide an important public service by ensuring that we're making decisions based on facts rather than fiction.

SETTING THE AGENDA

Every day, news organizations make decisions about what stories to cover and how much attention to give them. In doing so they're declaring what issues are important and need to be discussed by the public and decision-makers like governments.

Children's shoes and toys sit on the steps of the British Columbia Parliament Buildings to honor the Indigenous children who died at Canada's residential schools. After the unmarked graves of 215 residential school students were found near Kamloops, BC, in 2021, many people criticized newspapers for not immediately making the sad news the main story on the front page.
TAMASV/SHUTTERSTOCK.COM

This is a big responsibility, and media outlets don't always get it right. For example, the media largely ignored climate change for decades before finally starting to do a better job of covering it. On the flip side, news organizations can raise important issues that otherwise wouldn't have received any attention. For instance, in 2019 the CBC did an investigation into minor sports coaches who abused children, making many more people aware of the issue and leading to policies to protect kids.

THE WATCHDOGS

Journalists are called *watchdogs* because they keep a close eye on powerful people and speak up when they do something wrong, just like a dog guards its person's property and barks when there are intruders.

The most important people journalists keep tabs on are elected officials like the president of the United States, the prime minister of Canada and your local mayor. This is because elected officials are chosen by and work for the public, the decisions they make can significantly affect our lives and they spend and are paid with *public money*. By holding people in power to account, journalists protect *democracy*.

Journalists also keep an eye on business leaders, celebrities and people in positions of trust, such as teachers, sports coaches and doctors. Like politicians, these people can influence and affect our lives.

If a journalist suspects a powerful person has done something wrong, they may investigate the matter and report on it if they have enough evidence. When people find out about

EXTRA! EXTRA!

Sixty percent of teens say following the news helps them have a good understanding of what's going on in the world, and 41 percent say it helps them feel prepared to make a difference in their communities.

—Common Sense Media,
Teens and the News 2020

powerful people behaving badly, they may demand action. If a reporter reveals that a person may have committed a crime, the police may do their own investigation and charge the individual, starting the process of getting justice for those who were harmed. For example, there have been several cases of parent volunteers stealing from minor sports organizations. In some cases, journalists were the first to report on these crimes, leading parents and kids to demand action, police to investigate and judges to send the scammers to jail.

CONVERSATION STARTERS

News organizations provide an important forum for exchanging information and ideas. They should share opposing views on issues, like the arguments for and against building a new recreation center. They should also cover the concerns of all members of their communities, like how homeowners and people who are homeless feel about a new shelter going up in their neighborhood. However, as you'll learn in chapters 3 and 4, they don't always do these things because they're trying to push a certain side of a story or don't have enough time to explore all angles.

KAT BERBARI/STREET ROOTS

STAR REPORTER:
JANNA TAMIMI

Janna Tamimi, who goes by the name Janna Jihad, became the world's youngest journalist in 2014 when, at the age of seven, she started reporting on the Israeli-Palestinian conflict. Palestine and Israel have been fighting over land for decades, and children have seen a lot of violence and even been hurt or killed. The Palestinian girl decided to become a journalist after her cousin and uncle were killed and she realized there wasn't enough media coverage of what was happening in Palestine and how it affected children. Janna films clashes, raids and arrests in her village and then posts her reports on her Facebook page, where she has more than 600,000 followers. She shows how her rights and the rights of other children are being violated and how they can't have a normal childhood.

"I want to be the voice of those children...and to raise awareness about this very important international issue. My camera is my weapon of choice." —Janna Tamimi

Media outlets often invite the public to weigh in on issues by calling in, writing letters, commenting on stories or attending events. People also talk about the news with their friends, family members, colleagues and neighbors, which may lead to new ideas and solutions to challenges big or small.

FINDING SOLUTIONS

In 2022 the CBC published a story about a high-school teacher in Surrey, British Columbia, who launched a plant project to help her students cope with anxiety. Each student grows and cares for their own plant. They can put it on their desk if they're having a hard day, and they can share their worries with it when they're watering it. The project is based on the Persian concept of sang-e saboor, which means that confiding in a person or object can take away your sorrow. By sharing this story,

BEHIND THE HEADLINES

Most people have to pay tax based on how much money they make. Governments collect this money and use it to pay for important things like building schools and hospitals and fighting climate change and pandemics. But some people try to avoid paying taxes by hiding their money in **tax havens**. In 2016 a team of more than 350 journalists from 80 countries revealed that 140 politicians, celebrities, business leaders, suspected criminals and other powerful people were doing just that.

It all started when a **whistleblower** gave two journalists 11.5 million confidential documents from a law firm in Panama. The journalists shared the information with the International Consortium of Investigative Journalists, which then assembled the team that looked into it. As a result of the investigation, which became known as the *Panama Papers*, police raided the law firm and arrested its founders. The prime minister of Iceland, a minister in Spain and a city council chairman in Mongolia resigned, and Pakistan's prime minister was sent to jail for corruption. Several Chinese politicians were named in the papers, but the government, which doesn't respect press freedom, banned journalists from writing about the issue. Authorities in other countries made new rules and recouped more than $1.3 billion by 2021, all thanks to the whistleblower and the journalists.

the CBC encouraged other teachers to try this approach, which could help more kids manage their anxiety.

Media outlets often share solutions to problems through their reporting rather than only focusing on problems. This is called solutions journalism, and it's becoming increasingly popular. When journalists share solutions, the public and decision-makers can learn about, consider and implement them.

GIVING VOICE TO THE VOICELESS

It can be difficult for some people in our society to speak up and be heard by people in power. News outlets give voice to the voiceless by reporting on issues that affect groups like children, people who are poor and people who are in jail. This helps ensure that the human rights of all people are protected.

For example, when former US president Donald Trump implemented a "zero-tolerance" immigration policy in 2018, resulting in a growing number of **undocumented migrants** being detained at the United States–Mexico border, journalists wrote hundreds of stories about how government officials were mistreating migrants, including children, and violating their human rights. Some children were separated from their parents, held in cages and denied food, beds and toys. The media attention led to greater awareness of the issue, which in turn led to protests, calls for actions and, eventually, the release of the children and their reunification with their parents.

KEEPING YOU SAFE

The news is critical in times of emergencies like natural disasters and public health crises. News outlets warn people about dangers and keep them up to date as situations change.

Students at a school in Surrey, BC, paint plant pots as part of a project to help them manage anxiety. The project was featured in the news, allowing other people to learn about it and potentially do something similar.
BEN NELMS/CBC

Children and adults participate in a protest against US immigration policies outside a government building in New York in 2018.
SPENCER PLATT/GETTY IMAGES

A reporter covers a California wildfire in 2020, sharing important information about evacuation orders and helping keep people safe.

For example, during the 2021 wildfire season in British Columbia and the western United States, people relied on the media to keep them informed of evacuation orders as the flames moved in on their homes. And during the COVID-19 pandemic, journalists kept us up to date on outbreaks, school closures and rules for hanging out with our friends.

FOR THE HISTORY BOOKS

Want to know what the biggest news was on the day you were born? Or who won the Stanley Cup for the past three decades? Or perhaps how the world reacted when the first iPhone hit the market? Look it up on the internet or at the library. Thanks to journalists, you're likely to find the answers you're looking for.

News organizations document history for future generations, allowing people to learn from the past and build a better future. Every day journalists generate a massive amount of information about our world. Historians review and analyze this information and use it to write history books like that textbook you're using in social studies.

ENTERTAINMENT VALUE

"15 Poop Horror Stories That Will Make You Feel Better about Yourself." "20 Facts about the Original 'The Lion King' That You Probably Didn't Know Until Today." "21 People Share the Funniest Things They've Ever Heard a Kid Say." These are all real headlines from the online media outlet BuzzFeed, showing that journalism can entertain as well as inform and educate.

In fact, most media outlets strive to entertain their audiences. If they didn't, a lot of people probably wouldn't bother tuning in. This is why you'll often see light stories among all the heavy news. Serious news can be entertaining too. In fact, many books and movies are based on real-life news stories. The Panama Papers even inspired a Netflix movie called *The Laundromat* starring Academy Award–winning actors.

EXTRA! EXTRA!

In the early days of the COVID-19 pandemic, people flocked online to get the latest news. In the United States people spent three times as much time reading the news on mobile devices in March 2020 compared with March 2019.

—Nielsen Media Research

THREE
Making the News

WHAT'S NEWS?

All kinds of things can be news. Good things, bad things. Happy things, sad things. Serious things, silly things. All of these things fall into different categories, such as local news, national news, international news, sports, business and entertainment. If you flip through a newspaper, navigate around an online news site or tune in to a radio or TV news broadcast, you may notice that it's organized into sections or segments based on categories. There are also specialty media outlets that exclusively cover certain subjects such as gardening, golf and even video games. Journalists often specialize in specific subject areas. Passionate about skiing and

Newspapers often have several sections, which make them perfect for sharing with your friends or family members.
TDOES/SHUTTERSTOCK.COM

There are magazines about all kinds of subjects, including homes, health and hairstyles.

NILOO/SHUTTERSTOCK.COM

soccer? You could become a sports reporter! Love music and movies? Becoming an arts reporter could be in your future!

NEWS VERSUS OPINION

News is factual information that's been collected and verified by journalists. Many media outlets also publish opinion, which is what people think about the news or other issues.

Opinion articles can take many forms. Editorials are articles in which publications or journalists express their opinions. Op-eds (short for "opposite the editorial page") are articles in which an individual or a group expresses their opinions. There are also advice columns, in which an author offers advice to someone who writes in with a problem, and reviews, in which an author reviews a product like a book or a business like a restaurant.

It's important to know how to tell news and opinion apart. Fortunately, it's pretty easy. Most publications label

opinion articles. Opinion pieces may also include the author's photo and a short biography. And the article will likely include personal statements like "I believe," and "We think."

EDITORIAL VERSUS ADVERTORIAL

"America's Smartphone Obsession Extends to Mobile Banking." That was a headline published on the news website *GoUpstate* in 2015. The story was about how more and more Americans are banking through mobile apps. It included stats from a Bank of America survey, quotes from a Bank of America employee and information on the Bank of America app. The catch? The story was an advertorial for the Bank of America.

Advertorials often look very similar to news stories. Try to spot advertorials by looking for words likes *advertisement*, *paid post* or *special promotional feature* at the top or bottom of the page.

URBANCOW/GETTY IMAGES

Advertorials are advertisements that look like news stories. They are labeled as ads at the top or bottom of the page, but sometimes the wording is unclear. They may say *sponsored*, *branded content*, *special promotional feature* or something similar.

Many people think advertorials are deceptive and make it difficult for readers to tell what's an ad and what's real news. A Boston University study found that 90 percent of people who read the Bank of America advertorial thought it was a news article.

Advertorials are becoming increasingly popular for a few reasons. First, they're often more effective than traditional ads. Second, as media outlets close or cut journalists, organizations are having a harder time getting media attention. And third, advertorials provide media outlets with a much-needed source of revenue.

Many organizations have skipped advertorials and gone straight to creating their own publications. *Costco Connection*, for example, is a magazine packed with stories that promote products and services sold by the company. A story about *PAW Patrol*'s popularity and positive impact on kids, for instance, mentioned the *PAW Patrol* toys, books and clothing available at Costco.

MEDIA'S HIDDEN BIAS

Many news organizations are biased. They choose what stories to cover and how to cover them based on their social, political, environmental or economic beliefs. However, they usually don't declare their bias, which isn't fair to news consumers.

Some people choose to consume biased news because it supports their views. Other people follow such news thinking it's impartial and may change their opinions based on the information.

Some experts say biased news makes us less informed and less tolerant of different people and ideas. They think media outlets should declare their bias and people should look to a variety of news sources to get diverse perspectives. Some organizations, such as AllSides and Ad Fontes Media, have created media bias charts to help you figure out where media outlets sit on the *political spectrum*. I also have some tips in chapter 6 on how you can become a critical news consumer.

AllSides™ Media Bias Chart™

All ratings are based on online content only — not TV, print, or radio content.
Ratings do not reflect accuracy or credibility; they reflect perspective only.

L	L	C	R	R
	AP			BRETBART B
BuzzFeed News	CBS	BBC	NEW YORK POST news	DAILY CALLER
CNN	NBC	Newsweek	The Post Millennial.	DAILY WIRE
HUFFPOST		REUTERS	THE WALL STREET opinion JOURNAL	
msnbc	The New York news Times	REAL CLEAR POLITICS	Examiner	FOX NEWS channel
THE NEW YORKER				NATIONAL REVIEW
The New York opinion Times	npr	THE HILL	The Washington Times	NEW YORK POST opinion
	USA TODAY	THE WALL STREET news JOURNAL		
	The Washington Post			

L LEFT   L LEAN LEFT   C CENTER   R LEAN RIGHT   R RIGHT

AllSides Media Bias Ratings™ are based on multi-partisan, scientific analysis.
This is a simplified version of the chart. Visit AllSides.com for the full chart.

AllSides Media Bias Chart™ (Version 6)

© 2022, ALLSIDES.COM. USED WITH PERMISSION.

FAMILIES REUNITED AT BORDER!

BREAKING NEWS

WHAT MAKES THE NEWS?

Why do some stories get lots of coverage while others get none? Journalists cover news that people need and want to know because it's important or interesting. They consider several factors when determining if a story is **newsworthy**. Here are a few.

When Did It Happen?

News stories are like cookies—they're better when they're fresh and can get stale after a while. Have you ever noticed that the word *news* has *new* in it? New events and information are more newsworthy because they just happened. A story in the community paper about your team winning the championship is a lot more interesting right after the event than in the following month.

Where Did It Happen?

We're generally more interested in news that happens close to us because it affects us more. A meteorite landing in Africa is cool, but a meteorite (safely) landing in your neighborhood is *really* cool.

EXTRA! EXTRA!

Three-quarters of people prefer news that reflects a range of views and lets them decide what to think.

—*Reuters Institute Digital News Report 2021*

How Many People Did It Affect?

Have you heard of Q fever? How about COVID-19? Q fever is an infectious disease just like COVID-19, but it hasn't started a global pandemic. The more people affected by an issue, the more likely it is to make the news.

Is There Conflict?

As you may have learned in school, stories are better if they have conflict. Big news events like elections and criminal trials often have conflict, and so can many issues in your community like where to put a new garbage dump or bike lanes.

Is It Surprising?

There's an old saying in journalism that goes something like this: "When a dog bites a man, it's not news. But if a man bites a dog, it's news." In other words, the more surprising a story is, the more likely it is to make the news. (There have actually been several stories in the news about people biting dogs!)

It's important to be aware that when media outlets feature surprising news, it can make you think rare events happen more often than they really do. There's another expression in the media business along the lines of this: "You never read about a plane that didn't crash." Plane crashes are tragic events but fortunately they're extremely rare.

Does It Involve Prominent People?

If you dye your hair pink, it's unlikely to make the news. (But I bet it looks awesome!) If US President Joe Biden dyes his hair pink, it would be front-page news for days,

MONKEY BUSINESS IMAGES/
SHUTTERSTOCK.COM

BEHIND THE HEADLINES

In 2020, 13-year-old California girl Madeleine Fugate started the COVID Memorial Quilt to remember those who have died due to the disease. She collected quilt squares from people around the world who have lost loved ones, and sewed the squares onto panels. On the project website Madeleine explained how media coverage of the pandemic inspired her. "When you watch the news, it's just about the numbers and how they keep going up. They have gotten so high that we don't think of those numbers as people anymore, and I want to change that." Madeleine's story, which is a great example of a human-interest story, was featured in dozens of major media outlets. All the media attention helped more people learn about the project and encouraged mourning families to send in squares. Panels of the quilt have gone on to be displayed in museums, churches, universities and art galleries to encourage public mourning and healing.

Many news outlets have apps that send people notifications when there's breaking news.

OATAWA/GETTY IMAGES

with every angle explored. Why did he do it? How did he do it? What does it mean? Will it inspire other people to dye their hair pink?

Prominent people such as politicians, famous actors and professional athletes are more likely to make the news than everyday folks because people are more interested in what they're up to.

Is It Relevant to the Audience?

Different media outlets have different audiences, and journalists always need to make sure the news they share is relevant to their audience. A story about new sneakers made out of recycled materials may be a good fit for fashion and sports magazines but not for home and garden magazines—unless, of course, the shoes are compostable.

Does It Have Human Interest?

Even though people love celebrity news, they're also interested in stories about regular people overcoming obstacles or accomplishing amazing things. These stories often bring out our emotions and help us connect with the news and the people involved.

EXTRA! EXTRA!

TV news hosts are also known as *anchors*, but it's not because they "hold down" the show like an anchor holds down a ship. The term actually comes from relay racing and the anchor leg, which is the last leg of the race and is typically run by the fastest or most experienced member of the team.

38

WHO PUTS TOGETHER THE NEWS?

Making the news is like a big group project every day. Every media outlet has a different team of players, but there is some overlap. Here are some of the key jobs.

EDITORS
plan, oversee, review and revise the work of reporters.

FACT-CHECKERS
check the facts in stories and correct any errors.

REPORTERS
research issues, gather information, interview sources and produce stories.

PHOTOGRAPHERS AND VIDEOGRAPHERS
capture images to help tell stories.

HOSTS
present the news and interview people on TV, radio and podcasts.

PRODUCERS
work behind the scenes to get TV, radio and podcast shows on the air.

CBC News Network host Aarti Pole prepares for a broadcast in Toronto. Behind the scenes, several producers, camera operators, sound technicians and other team members help get the show on the air.

AARTI POLE

WHERE DOES THE NEWS COME FROM?

The news comes from all kinds of different places. Sometimes it's out in the open, and other times it's buried and journalists have to dig it up.

Events

Major world events like wars and the Olympics are easy to spot and lead to a lot of coverage. Local media outlets often cover events in our own backyards, such as festivals and fires.

Announcements

News also comes from organizations like universities, nonprofits and governments. A university may be publishing a new study on how much sleep kids *really* need, a nonprofit may be launching a campaign to save the endangered red panda and a government may be announcing a new holiday.

These organizations often invite reporters to events called news conferences to make their announcements and take questions from reporters. Organizations may also send out news releases, which are documents that outline their news and include comments from their representatives.

Investigations

Media organizations also do investigations to uncover news that is hidden intentionally or unintentionally. Sometimes investigations start after reporters receive tips from the public or other sources. For instance, in 2016, nine-year-old reporter Hilde Kate Lysiak got a tip that there had been a murder in her hometown of Selinsgrove, Pennsylvania. She was first to break the news, beating all the other outlets.

Sometimes people don't want to share information with reporters because it reveals things they'd rather keep secret. When public organizations like schools, police departments and governments don't hand over the infor-mation reporters want, those reporters can make freedom of information requests, which are formal processes to ask for information. Sometimes news organizations have to pay for the information and wait a very long time for it. There are certain types of information organizations won't release, such as documents that invade people's privacy or threaten national security.

Going Undercover

Perhaps the most exciting way to get a scoop is to go under-cover. To do this, a journalist may pretend to be someone else

hidden
camera

to gain access to people or places and get the information they want.

For example, in 2018 journalists from the CBC's investigative news show *Marketplace* posed as customers at several trampoline parks across Canada to see if the parks were safe. Using hidden cameras, they discovered that staff often don't enforce the rules—such as one kid per trampoline, no double bouncing and no belly flops into the foam pit—and that kids often seriously hurt themselves.

FOLLOW THE RULES

Anyone can call themselves a journalist and publish news. Journalists don't have to pass any tests or get a license or a certificate to do their job, unlike other professionals such as teachers, doctors and lawyers.

However, many news organizations and professional journalism associations have their own sets of standards and codes of ethics. The guidelines vary, but here are some of the most common and important ones.

Tell the Truth

Journalists should make sure that the facts they report are accurate, all sides are fairly presented and all the information is in **context**. For example, if a reporter is covering a story about a heat wave, they should explain how such extreme weather events are becoming more common due to climate change.

If journalists make mistakes, they should correct them as soon as possible and let people know by printing or broadcasting corrections. Sometimes corrections can be the most entertaining part of the news. Brazilian news magazine *Veja* once apologized after mistakenly saying that a presidential candidate likes to watch *Toy Story* in his free time. He actually said he likes to read the work of famous author Leo Tolstoy. Whoops!

Treat People Fairly

Journalists should treat everyone involved in the news fairly and respect their rights. For example, journalists should always give people and organizations accused of doing something bad the chance to respond to those accusations.

Journalists should show compassion to people who are affected by the news and respect their privacy. For example, they shouldn't continually knock on the door of someone who has lost a loved one in a tragic accident.

Journalists should take special care when interviewing, photographing or filming children and always get a parent's or guardian's permission first. Kids are often not aware of the implications of being in the media. If you make a funny comment on the TV news, it could go viral and be on the internet forever!

Act Independently

Journalists should maintain independence from the people they cover and avoid ***conflicts of interest***. This means they shouldn't report on stories that include their friends or

LEO TOLSTOY

SASS, MOSCOW/WIKIMEDIA COMMONS/ PUBLIC DOMAIN

family members or organizations they're involved in. It would be unethical for me, for example, to write a story about a fundraiser for my kids' skating club.

Journalists should also refuse to be influenced by powerful people and advertisers. For instance, if a video-game maker places an ad in a kids' magazine and asks the editor to write a positive review about the game, the editor should (politely) tell the video-game maker to buzz off.

Be Impartial

Journalists shouldn't let their opinions get in the way of fair and accurate reporting and should cover all legitimate sides of stories fairly. For instance, if a journalist is covering a story about cellphone bans in schools but strongly believes kids should have access to their devices, they should still fairly cover the arguments for and against bans and not let their personal opinion influence the story.

However, some journalists have challenged this rule, saying it's impossible to be impartial because everyone has a point of view. They think it's better to declare their perspective rather than try to be impartial. Some journalists and news consumers also think certain issues don't need to be covered from all angles. For instance, since nearly all climate scientists agree human activity is causing climate change, some people think stories about the topic don't need to include the thoughts of those who disagree.

PETER DAZELEY/GETTY IMAGES;
TETRA IMAGES/TGI/GETTY IMAGES

WHO IS WATCHING THE WATCHDOGS?

The media is good at keeping an eye on powerful people and organizations and pointing out their mistakes, but who is watching the watchdogs?

44

If you have a complaint about a story in the media, you can contact the outlet to tell them what you think. Many media outlets have public editors or ombudspersons who accept and investigate complaints. If you don't hear back or you're not happy with their response, you may be able to contact a news council or broadcast commission. These organizations investigate complaints from the public about media outlets that have allegedly broken their codes of conduct. However, they typically only investigate outlets that have voluntarily joined their organizations, and not all regions have councils or commissions.

There are also media critics—journalists who write about the media—though they are becoming rarer as outlets are forced to cut back.

COURTESY OF JESSE BROWN

STAR REPORTER:
JESSE BROWN

When Jesse Brown was in high school in the mid-1990s, he launched a magazine called *Punch*. After he polled students on their favorite teachers and published the results, the principal banned the magazine and threatened to expel the **cub reporter**. The story got out to the media, and Jesse and the principal went on the radio to argue their sides. Jesse ended up winning a student journalism award for investigative reporting and went on to become a professional journalist and media critic.

Early in his career, he pranked other journalists by pitching them fake stories and then writing about it to show how they failed to verify that the news was accurate. For one prank he put out a press release about a fake computer program called Baby Speak that allowed Canadian babies to communicate with tots in other countries. A local TV news station fell for the prank and did a story on Baby Speak.

In 2013, after noticing a lack of media criticism in Canada, Jesse launched his own podcast, called *Canadaland*, to keep tabs on the industry. Since then *Canadaland* has grown to be a news site and podcast network that covers media, current affairs and politics. In 2021 more than 10,000 people pitched in over $60,000 a month to help support the media outlet, showing just how much people want to hear media criticism.

"Powerful people and institutions need to be held accountable by journalists, but who holds journalists accountable? The media is itself very powerful and we have to investigate it, question it and criticize it." —Jesse Brown

FOUR
Press under Pressure

BROKEN BUSINESS MODEL

News organizations and journalists face lots of challenges today, many of which have been brought on or intensified by the internet and social media.

Most media outlets make money by selling subscriptions and advertising space, but the internet and social media have challenged that *business model*. Here's how.

Subscriptions

In the early days of online news, most media outlets put their stories online for free. As a result, many people cancelled their newspaper and magazine subscriptions because they wanted to save money and trees, and they preferred to read the news online. Some outlets later put up *paywalls*, but people were used to getting the news for free, so many of them just went to free news sites.

Advertising

Advertisers have followed readers online, but they're buying most of their ad space from Google and Facebook rather than directly from media outlets. Many advertisers prefer to buy ad space from these big tech companies because they often charge less than media outlets, have massive audiences and allow advertisers to target certain consumers. For instance, if Nintendo places an ad on Facebook, it can choose the age, gender, location and interests of the people who see it.

The internet has also led to the decline of paid classified ads, which are short ads that people and businesses place for everything from used toys to jobs. Today most people prefer to place ads on free classified websites like Craigslist, Kijiji and Facebook Marketplace.

Many people put up signs saying they don't want free community newspapers.
ALENAKRAVCHENKO/DREAMSTIME.COM

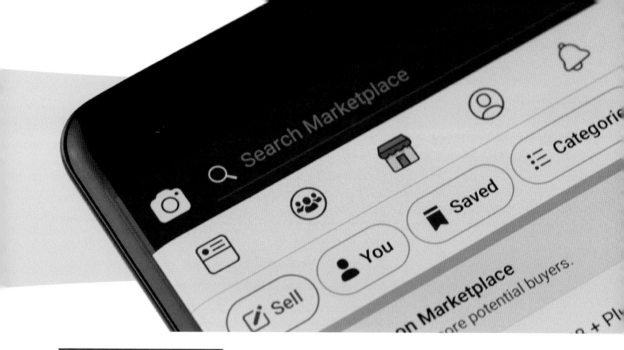

BIG TECH'S FREE RIDE

Every day, millions of people go to Google and Facebook to search and scroll for news. This allows the tech companies to sell a huge amount of ad space because so many people are visiting their websites. Google and Facebook also allow media outlets to share their stories with massive audiences for free. The tech companies claim this is a fair trade, but many media outlets disagree. These outlets say the tech companies are using their content to sell ad space while taking advertising dollars away from them.

Around the world, news organizations have joined forces to demand their governments take action to level the playing field. In 2021 Australia became the first country to pass a law forcing Google and Facebook to pay for news.

Meanwhile, the tech companies have launched programs to help news organizations address their challenges, and new media outlets that don't rely on subscriptions or advertising are finding success. You'll read about some of those outlets in chapter 5.

The growth of online marketplaces, like Facebook Marketplace, has led to the decline of classified ads in newspapers.
PIXIEME/SHUTTERSTOCK.COM

CHASING EYEBALLS

If you play sports, you know that competition can be good. It can drive you to work hard to improve and always try your best. But too much competition can be bad. It can push people to take cheap shots to win at any cost.

News outlets have always been competitive, but the internet has pushed their rivalry to a new level. There are a couple of reasons for this. Outlets have always wanted to be first to publish stories because doing so is like winning a race, and the internet allows them to publish their stories as soon as they're ready rather than waiting to share them on the six o'clock news or in the paper the next day. Publishing stories first—and publishing stories people really want to read—attracts more people to news organizations' websites. This allows them to sell more advertising because advertisers always want their ads to be seen by as many people as possible. However, when outlets are busy chasing eyeballs, they don't have as much time to produce quality journalism. This can lead to the following three issues.

Sloppy Work

Media outlets often rush to publish their stories first. But you probably know what happens when you rush through your schoolwork—you don't do it as well as when you take your time, and you may make mistakes. Many experts say the creation of online news has led to a decrease in the quality of news and an increase in the number of errors.

Clickbait

Many media outlets now produce clickbait, which is content—headlines and teaser text—designed to attract

In 2021 nearly 100 newspapers across Canada, including the *Montreal Gazette*, ran blank front pages to draw attention to the impact Google and Facebook are having on journalism and democracy by gobbling up the majority of advertising revenue.

your attention and get you to click on links. Unfortunately, clickbait often over-promises and under-delivers and is sometimes even false or misleading. For example, the British *Telegraph* shared a headline on social media in 2016 that read "Mysterious chimpanzee behaviour could prove they believe in God, according to scientists," but the story itself had little proof.

Sensational Stories

"If it bleeds, it leads." This grim expression in journalism means that bad news involving conflict, violence and injury gets featured prominently because people are more interested in it than in good news. However, several studies have found that consuming too much bad news can harm your mental health. Research also shows that people are less likely to trust news outlets if their coverage is always negative, especially if it doesn't reflect people's daily lives.

HOW DO TEENS FEEL ABOUT THE NEWS?

Data Source:
commonsensemedia.org

POSITIVE FEELINGS

Informed: 37 percent
Motivated: 12 percent
Energized: 7 percent

NEGATIVE FEELINGS

Frustrated: 45 percent
Confused: 30 percent
Worn out: 25 percent

A SPOOKY SITUATION

When newspapers and magazines lose advertisers and subscribers, they don't have as much money to operate. As a result, many of them have laid off journalists, reduced their *circulation* or shut down entirely. Research shows that between 2004 and 2019, more than a quarter of US newspapers closed and more than half of US journalists lost their jobs. This has led to ghost newspapers and news deserts.

Ghost newspapers are ghosts of their former selves, with fewer journalists and readers. They don't cover as many stories as they used to, they don't cover stories as well as they used to and they don't cover some subjects at all. For example, lots of community newspapers have stopped covering minor sports and school boards, meaning issues that you and your family may care about aren't getting any attention.

News deserts are communities that have lost their newspapers and now have very limited access to local news. Research shows that people who live in news deserts are less likely to vote, volunteer and even trust their neighbors.

PLAYING MONOPOLY

In the early days of the media industry, individuals or small companies owned most media outlets. But over time many media outlets got bought by bigger and bigger companies. Today *media conglomerates* own the majority of newspapers, magazines and TV and radio stations in North America. In 2018 just 25 companies owned a third of all newspapers in the United States.

This media *monopoly* is a problem because it means that a few big companies control the information that we get. It also means that decisions about local media outlets are being made by people who don't have strong ties to those communities. These giant corporations typically prioritize profit over people and good journalism, often laying off journalists and closing media outlets in order to make more money. And when people don't have access to local news, they may go to social media or other sources for the news and find false or misleading information.

FAKE NEWS

Did you see the story about how California theme parks banned screaming when they reopened in 2021 after COVID-19 closures? "No screaming on California roller coasters and thrill rides, state guidelines say," screamed a headline in the *Orange County Register*. A YouTuber made a video about the alleged ban, complete with a photo of the newspaper headline, and the story went viral. But it turns out the headline was misleading. The story actually reported that the California Attractions and Parks Association's Responsible Reopening Plan said theme parks should take steps to limit—not ban—shouting on rides.

Fake news is false or misleading information presented as news. You may come across fake news on websites that look like real news sites or on social media sites. The internet has made it possible for anyone to create a "news" website, and social media allows fake news to spread like a lice outbreak in a kindergarten class.

People who produce fake news may want to further their own cause, hurt other people or make more money through advertising. Anyone can put Google ads on their website and collect cash based on the number of people who visit.

When community newspapers are purchased by media conglomerates, readers often notice changes, like a lack of coverage of local events.
FABIO PRINCIPE / EYEEM/GETTY IMAGES

EXTRA! EXTRA!

Many teens look to social media for news.
- 77 percent get news and headlines from social media.
- 39 percent "often" get news from personalities, influencers and celebrities on social media and YouTube.
- 28 percent say their "preferred" news source is personalities, influencers and celebrities on social media and YouTube.

—Common Sense Media, *Teens and the News 2020*

Rioters storm the Capitol Building in Washington, DC, in 2021, while police and security work to hold them back. More than 900 people were arrested and charged for their actions during the attack.

BRENT STIRTON/GETTY IMAGES

Real Consequences

Fake news can have real consequences. For example, in the lead up to the 2016 US presidential election, several Russian companies and individuals created and spread fake news to persuade people to vote for Republican Donald Trump and dissuade them from voting for Democrat Hillary Clinton. The fake news included stories that Clinton was in very poor health and the Pope supported Trump. And it may have worked. An Ohio State University study suggested that this fake news played a role in Trump's win.

Trump then became famous for calling real news that was critical of him "fake news" and spreading lies himself in media interviews and speeches and on social media. For instance, he repeatedly falsely claimed that the 2020 election, which he lost to Democrat Joe Biden, was "stolen." This prompted thousands of Trump supporters to attack the Capitol Building in Washington, DC, on Jan. 6, 2021, and disrupt the US Congress, which was in the process of affirming the presidential election results. At least five people died due to the attack, and more than 140 police officers were injured. Several social media sites banned Trump after the attack.

It can be difficult to figure out what's real news and what's fake news, but I have some tips for you in chapter 6.

YOUNG JOO JUN/THE AQUINIAN

STAR REPORTER:
DANIEL DALE

Daniel Dale is famous for fact-checking politicians. After former Toronto mayor Rob Ford falsely accused him of standing on bricks to peer over his fence and take photos of his children, Dale realized that journalists need to call out politicians when they lie so people aren't misled. (Ford later admitted he was fibbing and made a public apology to Dale, which the reporter accepted.) Dale went on to fact-check former US president Donald Trump for the *Toronto Star* and discovered that he made an average of six false statements per day in his first 835 days as president, telling tales about everything from wars to the weather. Dale even busted Trump lying about being told by the leader of the Boy Scouts of America that his 2017 National Jamboree speech was the greatest speech ever made to the organization. In 2019 Dale started fact-checking politicians for CNN.

"Lying in politics should be combatted aggressively." –Daniel Dale

IS THERE AN ECHO IN HERE?

These days most people get some news from social media. They often do this because it's convenient—they're already on social media looking at what their friends are up to, chiming in on group discussions or watching viral cat videos. But there are some big problems with getting your news from social media.

Social media companies track your every move online, collect **data** on you and feed that data into algorithms, which are systems that predict what you'd like to see on social media and then show it to you. Social media companies want to keep you on their sites as long as possible so they can put more ads in front of you and make more money.

If you stop scrolling through Facebook to click on a story about *The Avengers*, the site will put even more *Avengers* news in your feed. While that

You and your friends probably share a lot of interests and opinions. That's why you're friends! But if you get all your news from social media, you may miss out on facts and opinions that expand your mind and worldview.

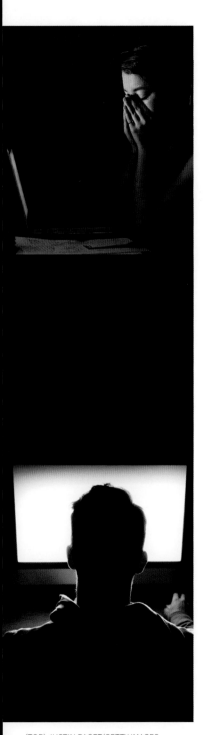

may sound awesome, it usually isn't a good thing. If you only see news about *The Avengers*, you may miss news about *Batman*. Similarly, if you only see stories about the economic reasons for cutting down trees, you may miss news about the environmental reasons for saving them, which could shape how you feel about the issue.

Another problem with relying on social media for news is that our friends often share our views and values. These friends will probably share news stories and commentary that we agree with and like what we share. This has created what experts call the *echo chamber*—an environment in which we only encounter information and opinions that reflect and reinforce our own. When people don't see opposing viewpoints, their beliefs can become even stronger and it can become even harder for them to see the other sides of the story.

TACKLING TROLLS

If you've ever been called a mean name or told your opinion is wrong, you know how bad it can feel. As you learned in chapter 1, many media outlets allow readers to comment on stories on their websites or social media pages. This has sparked many constructive conversations but has also led to many arguments, insults and even threats.

Some people post offensive or provocative comments just to make other people upset or angry because they find it entertaining. They often use fake names to conceal their identities. These people have become known as **trolls** for a couple of reasons. One, they behave like some storybook trolls—they're antisocial, they like to argue and they make life difficult for other people. And two, trolling is a fishing technique that involves dragging baited lines through the water.

Trolls troll the internet by leaving comments to bait people into debates.

While most media outlets have staff members who monitor the comments and delete the inappropriate ones, it can be tough to keep up. As a result, some media outlets have stopped allowing people to comment.

THE DIVERSITY DILEMMA

What do you think would happen if all the journalists working on your local radio news show were white men? The show would probably largely reflect the interests, perspectives and concerns of white men.

When newsrooms don't reflect the diversity in their communities, they may overlook important issues and points of view, and their coverage may be unfair and unbalanced. People may not trust the news or may tune it out, thinking it's not for them.

This is why it's important to have people of all ethnicities, gender identities, sexual orientations, ages, abilities, backgrounds and political beliefs working in newsrooms. But the journalism industry, like other powerful institutions, has been dominated by white men for a long time. This is due to sexism and racism. And when media organizations do employ women and racialized people, they often pay them significantly less than they pay white men.

Kids' views are also not well represented in the media. A 2020 survey of US teens found that 75 percent think the news media has no idea about the experiences of people their age, up from 67 percent in 2017. While this shows that the media is getting even worse at reflecting the lives of kids, the good news is there's a growing number of media outlets just for kids, which you'll learn more about in chapter 6.

Getting to the Source

Journalists are also much more likely to use white men, rather than women and racialized people, as expert sources. There are several reasons for this. Journalists are more likely to interview people who look like them and have similar backgrounds, and since the majority of journalists are white men, the majority of sources are white men. White men are also more likely to be leaders and **spokespersons** of organizations, and people in these positions are often the ones journalists want to interview. Meanwhile, women and racialized people are less likely to see themselves as experts on issues and accept interview requests. They are also more likely to face backlash (like mean comments on social media) for providing comments to the media.

The lack of diversity in newsrooms also means that people who are involved in news events may be treated unfairly.

Studies show that stories involving Black suspects of violence get more coverage than stories involving white suspects. Additionally, Muslim perpetrators of terrorism are more likely to be called "terrorists" than are white perpetrators of terrorism. And missing persons get much more media attention when they're white compared with when they're Indigenous, even though Indigenous people are far more likely to go missing.

Fortunately, many organizations and media outlets are trying to improve diversity in the news industry, which you will learn more about in chapter 5.

FIGHTING FOR PRESS FREEDOM

As you learned in chapter 1, countries started making laws guaranteeing press freedom back in 1766. Yet in 2021 press freedom was completely or partially blocked in more than 130 of 180 countries surveyed by Reporters Without Borders for its annual World Press Freedom Index.

Some national governments don't permit any press freedom and have total control over news. They do this to control the information citizens can access in order to influence how people think and act. The government of North Korea, for example, controls the only news agency in the country. It also blocks people from accessing the internet so they can't get online news from outside the country. Anyone who figures out how to access such news and looks at it could be sent to prison.

Authorities in other countries block press freedom in different ways. They may withhold information from journalists, refuse to speak with them about certain issues, restrict them from accessing news events and even arrest them just

EXTRA! EXTRA!
US newsroom employees are less diverse than workers overall. Seventy-seven percent of newsroom employees are non-Hispanic white compared with 65 percent of all workers. Sixty-one percent of newsroom employees are male compared with 53 percent of all workers.
—Pew Research Center analysis of US Census Bureau data, 2012–2016

Anti-logging activists march at Fairy Creek on Vancouver Island, BC, in 2021. When police started arresting activists, close-up photos like this weren't possible because police created an exclusion zone and wouldn't let journalists enter it.

for doing their jobs. For instance, during the arrests of anti-logging activists at Fairy Creek on Vancouver Island, British Columbia, in 2021, police restricted journalists to areas far from the action and even arrested a journalist along with the activists. The Canadian Association of Journalists and several media outlets challenged the restrictions in court and won.

DANGER AT WORK

Being a journalist can be dangerous. Journalists sometimes go into scary situations, just as police officers, firefighters and soldiers do. I've gone to the scenes of crimes, fires and protests. Many brave journalists go into war zones and disaster areas to bring people the news.

Journalists can also experience violence and intimidation on the job. Powerful people like politicians, leaders of criminal organizations and police officers sometimes don't want certain stories to get out to the public or are mad that they did, so they threaten, hurt, imprison or even kill journalists to keep them quiet or punish them. This happens all over the world but is much more common in countries that don't respect press freedom.

A photojournalist covers a protest in Colombia. Reporting on such events can be dangerous and stressful.

INDEX 2022	PRESS FREEDOM RANKING	GLOBAL SCORE
1	Norway	92.65
2	Denmark	90.27
3	Sweden	88.84
4	Estonia	88.83
5	Finland	88.42
19	Canada	81.74
42	United States	72.74
176	Myanmar	25.03
177	Turkmenistan	25.01
178	Iran	23.22
179	Eritrea	19.62
180	North Korea	13.92

[source: rsf.org/en/ranking]

Reporters Without Borders publishes an annual World Press Freedom Index. The index ranks 180 countries on the level of press freedom enjoyed by media and journalists and gives those countries a score out of 100.

Journalists can also face online harassment. Research shows that female journalists are more likely than male journalists to face this kind of abuse due to sexism and **misogyny**.

Violence and harassment, as well as reporting on upsetting stories, can harm journalists mentally as well as physically. They may experience anxiety, depression and **post-traumatic stress disorder** and not get the help they need to heal. Some journalists have quit the business or avoided covering certain stories because of the risks. This is a problem because it means important stories aren't being told.

Fortunately, there are several organizations working hard to protect journalists. For example, the Committee to

Protect Journalists works with world leaders to improve the working conditions for journalists, helps journalists when they're in danger and advocates for justice when journalists are imprisoned or killed.

LOSING TRUST

All of these challenges have put a lot of strain on newsrooms, forcing outlets to close or cut back and leading journalists to pursue other professions. This leaves the public with fewer and lower-quality news sources and therefore less information to help them make important decisions.

The journalists who remain are expected to do more with less. They are often overworked, exhausted and frustrated that they can't do their jobs like they used to. Some of them are forced to cut corners—not speaking to as many people for stories, for example, or not fact-checking what sources say. As a result, the news is often not as good as it used to be and people are losing trust in it.

Nearly half of Americans have noticed a decrease in the quantity and quality of news in their local newspaper, according to a 2018 Pew Research Center survey. Additionally, only 29 percent of Americans and 45 percent of Canadians trust the news, according to the *Reuters Institute Digital News Report 2021*.

Fortunately, lots of people and organizations are working hard on solutions to these challenges in an effort to make journalism better and rebuild people's trust in the media.

SPENCER PLATT/GETTY IMAGES

BEHIND THE HEADLINES

In 2020, in Minnesota, a white police officer killed a Black man named George Floyd by kneeling on his neck while arresting him for allegedly using counterfeit money to buy cigarettes. The murder set off protests against racism around the world.

In the United States, police detained or arrested more than 125 journalists who were covering the protests. Police hurt hundreds of others by physically attacking them and using tear gas, pepper spray and rubber bullets.

Meanwhile, newspaper editors made several controversial decisions about the protest coverage. For instance, editors at the *Pittsburgh Post-Gazette* barred Black reporter Alexis Johnson from covering the protests, claiming she showed bias when she published a tweet highlighting how the public reacts differently to matters depending on whether they involve mostly white or mostly Black people. Johnson said she was discriminated against because of her race, the staff union demanded the paper apologize to Johnson and put her back on the story, more than 3,000 readers wrote the paper to voice support for the journalist and several advertisers pulled their ads from the paper.

The protests led journalists and the public to call out racism in policing and in journalism and demand better treatment of racialized people.

FIVE
Saving Journalism

OUT WITH THE OLD, IN WITH THE NEWS

Journalists tend to be a dedicated and creative bunch, so many of them have come up with new ways of doing business. Two growing business models that are showing promise are nonprofits and co-operatives.

Nonprofits

Nonprofit news outlets don't have to generate profits for **shareholders**. Such outlets cover their expenses with donations from individuals, funding from foundations and/or revenue from advertising. Some nonprofit news outlets **crowdfund** to cover their costs in general or for specific stories, projects or positions. *The Tyee*, for example, an independent media outlet in British Columbia, has crowdfunded to hire new reporters and cover elections.

Journalists at *The Tyee* discuss a project at their Vancouver, BC, office. In 2021 about half of the publication's budget came from Tyee Builders, readers who donate money to support the publication.
JACKIE DIVES

CHEK MEDIA GROUP

Co-ops

Co-operatives, or co-ops for short, are collectively owned by a group of people who share the profits and have a say in the business operations. In 2020 the *Devil Strip* in Akron, Ohio, became the first reader-owned local news co-op in the United States. Others have since followed. Co-ops often allow readers to become shareholders and attend meetings at which they vote on big decisions like what stories journalists should prioritize. Even kids can become shareholders!

FIGHTING FAKE NEWS

It isn't always easy to tell the difference between real news and fake news, so several organizations

BEHIND THE HEADLINES

You can't buy much for two dollars—maybe a chocolate bar, a bouncy ball or a Pokémon card. But in 2009 the employees at CHEK News in Victoria, BC, bought their TV station for a couple of bucks and saved it from going off the air.

Earlier that year the previous owner, Canwest Global Communications, had put the popular local station up for sale. But when Canwest couldn't find a buyer, it announced it would be shutting down CHEK. The employees were devastated but determined to find a solution. Community members were also disappointed, and many called and wrote Canwest, asking it to reconsider. One fan even made T-shirts that said *Save CHEK News*. He sold nearly 1,500 of them and donated the money to a children's charity.

Inspired by the support, the employees pooled their money, found some investors and made Canwest an offer. (Even though they only paid $2 for the station, they needed to come up with $2.5 million to cover their costs while they rebuilt—that's a lot of Pokémon cards!) After a lot of negotiating, Canwest accepted their offer, and CHEK News became the first employee-owned TV station in North America.

When the deal closed, there were still about 400 unsold *Save CHEK News* T-shirts in stores, so the superfan got them back, printed a *D* at the end of *save* to make it *saved* and put them back on the shelves. They quickly sold out. Today CHEK is still on the air.

are working hard to help people. There are now more than 100 fact-checking projects in about 40 countries. There's even a fact-checking project for kids by kids called the MediaWise Teen Fact-Checking Network. These groups fact-check claims made by politicians and other prominent people, as well as stories that are going viral on the internet, and post their results online. Many fact-checking groups invite people to send in claims, so if you see something dodgy, send them a note.

Since a lot of fake news spreads on social media, these companies are also trying to spot it and stop it. Facebook and Instagram use independent fact-checkers to review and rate the accuracy of stories. If a fact-checker rates a piece of content as false, the social media sites push it down the newsfeed so fewer people see it, label it as false and notify people who try to share it. However, they do not remove the content because they say that would be contrary to free speech.

The Teen Fact-Checking Network investigates viral claims about everything from Archie Comics to zombie viruses and teaches kids media-literacy skills so they can fact-check on their own.
POYNTER INSTITUTE FOR MEDIA STUDIES

Story circles give people the opportunity to meet neighbors and journalists in their communities and share their perspectives on important issues.
RAWPIXEL/SHUTTERSTOCK.COM

MAKING A CONNECTION

Many media outlets are starting to involve their audiences in their work. This can help outlets better understand the issues that matter to people and do a better job of covering them. It can also help them build community and build trust. Here are a few ways they're doing it.

Story Circles

Just like circle time in kindergarten, story circles bring people together to sit in a circle and share their thoughts. Capital Public Radio in Sacramento, California, for example, held several story circles with diverse residents to discuss housing and then produced a podcast on the subject in 2017.

Reader Questions

Media outlets invite people to send in questions and use those questions to help them decide what stories to cover. For example, Nashville Public Radio created the *Curious Nashville* podcast to investigate people's questions about the city and region. One simple question about why a park was

named after Fred Douglas led city officials to realize that their predecessors had misspelled the name of former slave and abolitionist Frederick Douglass way back in 1935. The city quickly corrected the error.

Behind the Scenes

Curious about how the news is made? Media outlets are taking their audiences behind the scenes to meet their journalists and explain how and why they cover certain stories. *Hakai Magazine*, for instance, where I worked, has a special section in its newsletter called "Behind the Story" in which journalists share interesting tidbits about what it took to tell the story. The magazine also hosts events at which readers get to meet reporters and learn more about their stories.

MINORITY REPORT

Several organizations and media outlets have taken steps to improve the diversity of their staff and sources. In 2020, for example, the Canadian Association of Black Journalists and Canadian Journalists of Colour made seven calls to action to Canadian news organizations. These calls included hiring more journalists of color, consulting with racialized

Newsrooms are working hard to become more inclusive and diverse.

PEKIC/GETTY IMAGES

communities about news coverage and creating scholarship and mentorship opportunities for aspiring journalists of color.

Many media organizations are already answering the calls. In 2020 *Chatelaine* committed to ensuring that 40 percent of freelance stories are written by racialized people.

Some organizations have even created opportunities for kids. Since 2001 the Asian American Journalists Association has run JCamp, a six-day training camp that brings together culturally diverse high-school students from across the United States to learn from journalists and media leaders.

To improve source diversity, many organizations are training experts on how to work with the media and helping them promote their work. One of the ways they are doing this is by maintaining databases where journalists can search for diverse sources by area of expertise.

Media outlets are also encouraging reporters to use diverse sources, setting goals for source diversity and keeping track of their progress. For example, the editors at *Chemical & Engineering News* require reporters to input information about source diversity into a database. Every three

COURTESY OF CONNIE WALKER

STAR REPORTER:
CONNIE WALKER

When Connie Walker was in high school, she followed the media coverage of the murder of Pamela George, an Indigenous woman who was killed by two white men in Regina, SK, in 1995. But Walker, who is from the Okanese First Nation, noticed that there weren't any Indigenous reporters covering the case. So she decided to write a story about it for her high-school paper. She also decided to pursue journalism as a profession to ensure that Indigenous stories are covered by Indigenous reporters and get the attention they deserve. While she was still a journalism student, she hosted *Street Cents*, a CBC show for kids about consumer and media literacy. She continued working for the CBC, covering many important Indigenous issues, helping establish the network's Indigenous unit and producing an award-winning podcast series called *Missing & Murdered*, which investigated the unsolved cases of missing and murdered Indigenous women and girls (MMIWG). She then went on to launch *Stolen*, a podcast series that has explored the story of a missing Indigenous woman and Connie's own family's experience with the residential school system. Her work has brought a lot of attention to MMIWG and residential schools, which were long largely ignored by the media.

"These stories are so important, and I'm so committed to telling them. I feel the responsibility to help tell them." —Connie Walker

months the data is tabulated and the whole team comes together to discuss the results and what they could do better.

BRINGING NEWS INTO THE CLASSROOM

Have you learned about the media industry in school? If so, you're not alone. Media literacy is becoming a popular subject in schools as teachers realize that it's more important than ever. Sixty-nine percent of teens have learned how to tell the difference between news and opinion, 48 percent have learned how to fact-check a news story and 45 percent have learned how to identify news bias, according to a 2020 study by Common Sense Media.

Several media outlets are helping teachers bring news into the classroom by creating educational materials based on their content. The *New York Times*' Learning Network, for example, includes activities inspired by *Times* content like current-events lessons, news quizzes, writing prompts and crosswords.

Studying media literacy in school can help you become a savvy news consumer.

HILL STREET STUDIOS/GETTY IMAGES

LOOK ON THE BRIGHT SIDE

There's plenty of positive news out there, and there's a growing number of media outlets committed to sharing it. Some are entirely dedicated to looking on the bright side. *Positive News*, for example, is a magazine for good journalism about good things. Other outlets have created special sections for sunny stories.

When you're craving positive vibes, you can check out one of the many outlets that feature good news and find stories like the one about the boy who was named the ultimate Josh after winning a pool-noodle battle against other Joshes.

JAIDEN TRIPI/JOURNAL STAR

Solutions journalism, which you learned about in chapter 2, is also becoming more popular. There's even a magazine dedicated to solutions journalism (appropriately called *Yes!*) and an organization dedicated to spreading the practice (appropriately called the Solutions Journalism Network). The network trains journalists and shares solutions stories from around the world on its website to inform and inspire readers, so you can check it out anytime you feel down about the news.

GOING HIGH TECH

Some news organizations are also turning to technology to save money or hang on to their audiences. Here are a few ways they're doing it.

Robot Reporters

Meet Heliograf, Bertie and Cyborg, some of the most productive and precise journalists around. These robot reporters work at some of the biggest media outlets in the world. They automatically generate articles by using ***artificial intelligence (AI)*** software. Robot reporters excel at covering stories that involve a lot of numbers and statistics, like sports results, weather reports and company earnings. For example, Heliograf, a reporter at the *Washington Post*, covered the Olympics and the presidential election. Journalism leaders say robot reporters aren't taking jobs away from human journalists but are freeing people up to work on more complicated stories. The best part? Robot reporters don't make typos.

Artificial Intelligence

Media outlets use AI in other ways too—for instance, to scan data and alert them if there is something out of the ordinary, which could mean a juicy story. During the Olympics, the *Washington Post* set up alerts to let editors know if an event result was 10 percent above or below an Olympic record. The newspaper also uses AI software to moderate comments, transcribe interviews and identify fake photos.

Virtual Reality

It's one thing to read a story about hunger, but it's another to wait in a long food-bank line and see someone collapse due to hunger. Some innovative journalists are helping people step right into news stories through virtual reality. Just like a virtual-reality video game, you put on goggles and are virtually transported to another scene. Virtual-reality journalism helps people really understand and feel what it's like to be involved in news events, which can help them develop more empathy for those involved and inspire them to take action on the issues at hand.

Many media outlets use drones to get aerial video footage and photos from inaccessible or dangerous areas such as the scene of a toxic spill or a landslide.
THAMRONGPAT THEERATHAMMAKORN/ GETTY IMAGES

THE BIG BAILOUT

While some media outlets have figured out ways to stay afloat, others need some support or they're going to sink. Some people think more of our tax dollars should go toward supporting journalism since it's essential to our democracy. Other people think if media outlets get money from the government, they'll be less likely to produce stories that are critical of the government. While the debate continues, several governments have stepped up their support for journalism. In 2018, for instance, the Canadian government pledged CAD$600 million to support news outlets over five years. That's a massive sum of money, but there are also lots of things you can do to support the media industry that don't cost a cent.

EXTRA! EXTRA!

Many countries have public broadcasters, which are media outlets dedicated to providing accessible programming to all citizens. Many of these outlets receive funding from the government but are editorially independent, which means that their coverage isn't influenced or controlled by the state.

SIX
Become a News Hound

FIND THE NEWS FOR YOU

There are lots of things you can do to keep learning about journalism and help make the media industry better. You can start by following the news, thinking about it and discussing it with other people.

The first step is finding some media outlets that you like and trust. To do this, you can look at outlets' websites, read their "About Us" pages and check out a few stories. You can also ask a parent, teacher or another trusted adult in your life what they think about outlets you're considering. Once you know you've found a few reliable news sources, you can start following them regularly.

Lots of people and media organizations have created news outlets just for kids, which are great

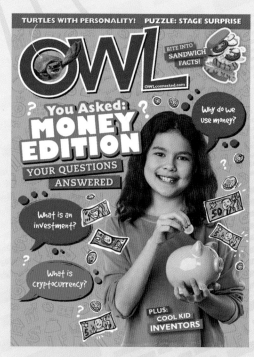

OWL is a magazine for preteens, packed with articles and activities that highlight a wide range of fascinating topics with an emphasis on science, technology, engineering, art and math.

OWL MAGAZINE. MAY 2022 ISSUE. USED WITH THE PERMISSION OF BAYARD CANADA, INC.

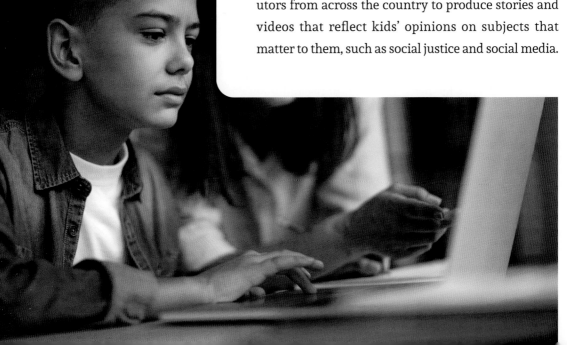

If you're unsure if something you're reading online is true, ask a trusted adult in your life or see if a fact-checking project has looked into it.

places to start. There are websites, magazines, TV news broadcasts and podcasts. These outlets:

- Cover top news stories in kid-friendly ways as well as hot topics that kids care about. For instance, one episode of *KidNuz*, a daily current affairs podcast, discussed the reopening of movie theaters after COVID restrictions lifted, flying cars and LEGO made from recycled plastic.

- Interview kids, invite them to share their thoughts and questions, and tell stories about cool kids doing cool things. For example, reporters for *NBC Nightly News with Lester Holt: Kids Edition*, a TV newscast that runs twice a week, has an "Ask the Doc" segment in which kids' health questions are answered by a doctor and an "Inspiring Kids" segment in which kids share their incredible accomplishments.

- Offer opportunities for kids to get involved in covering the news. For instance, *CBC Kids News*, a daily news service for kids, works with a team of teenage contributors from across the country to produce stories and videos that reflect kids' opinions on subjects that matter to them, such as social justice and social media.

You can find a list of media outlets for kids in the Resources section at the end of this book.

BECOME A CRITICAL NEWS CONSUMER

Have you ever heard the expression "Don't believe everything you read" (or see or hear)? It's important to keep this in mind even after you've found your favorite news sources. Here are some questions to help you determine if you can trust the news you're consuming.

- What kind of content are you consuming? Is it news, opinion or advertorial? Look for labels or listen for messages telling you what it is.
- Is the news outlet biased? Remember, some outlets choose what stories to cover and how to cover them based on their social, political, environmental or economic beliefs. Look up the outlet on one of the sites that monitors media bias.
- Who are the sources and why should you believe them? Are they government officials, experts or eye-witnesses? How do they know the information they're sharing? Do they have any motivation to want to make you believe a certain side of the story? Politicians, for instance, may want to influence your opinion to gain support for their plans and projects.
- What evidence is there to back up what sources are saying? If documents or studies are mentioned, where did they come from? There's a big difference between studies done by companies and those done by independent scientists. Did the journalist verify the evidence? If so, how?

BECOME A FAKE-NEWS DETECTIVE

It's also important to be on the lookout for fake news. Here are some questions to help you figure out if a news website or story is real or fake.

- Have you or the trusted adults in your life heard of the media outlet? If the site is new or unfamiliar, it may be a fake news site.
- Is there an "About Us" page with contact information? Reputable news sites will tell you who they are and how to get in touch with them, whereas fake news sites will be vague and misleading.
- Does the story include reputable quoted sources? Legitimate news stories quote officials and experts. If no one is quoted, or if you can't find out anything about the people who are quoted, the story may be fake.

Big news stories are often covered by several media outlets. If you see what seems like a major event being covered by only one outlet, it may be fake news.

MIHAJLO MARICIC / EYEEM/GETTY IMAGES

- Is the story being reported by other media outlets? Journalists love getting the scoop on breaking news, but if you don't see any other reputable media outlets following up on a big story, it may not be real.
- Does the story have lots of spelling and grammatical errors? Journalists strive to ensure their stories are free of such errors, but fake news outlets may not be as concerned.
- Does the story have a date on it? Real news sites always date their stories, but fake news sites often omit dates on their stories so they can promote them as news over and over again.
- Does the story have a **byline**? And if there's a photo, does it have a photo credit? Real news sites usually credit reporters and photographers. If this is missing, it may be a fake news story.
- Does the URL look funny? CBSnews.com.co, CNN-trending.com and Fox-news24.com were all fake news sites designed to look like real ones. It can

EXTRA! EXTRA!

Fifty-five percent of teens said they could tell if a news story was fake.

—Common Sense Media, *Teens and the News 2020*

sometimes be tough to spot these, but there are some clues. Real news sites use simple URLs without dots and dashes in the middle of names.

· If the story mentions "official" documents, are they real? Official documents from governments and other institutions can often be found online, so if you see something suspicious, you can check by looking up the organization or the document itself.

There are lots of online games and quizzes to help you practice your fake-news detective skills. Look for a list of them in the Resources section.

DEAR EDITOR

Remember Nellie Bly, the investigative journalist you met in chapter 1? After she wrote a letter to the editor of the *Pittsburgh Dispatch*, he hired her as a reporter. If you feel strongly about a story in the news or an issue you think should be in the news, you can write a letter too.

Most newspapers and magazines accept and publish letters to the editor. You can usually find these letters at the beginning or end of publications or on the editorial pages. You can also write or call in to TV and radio news shows. Some of them read or play these messages or speak with callers on air.

There are lots of reasons to write or call media outlets. You can share your thoughts with a large audience and influence public opinion. You can correct misinformation or misconceptions. And you can help create more awareness about issues that are important to you. Some of the best letters to the editor are written by kids because you have a unique perspective on the news that adults may have overlooked.

BEHIND THE HEADLINES

In 2018 the *Burnaby NOW* newspaper in British Columbia said the best letter to the editor it had received all year was from a teenager. Twelfth-grade student Anna Schillaci-Ventura wrote the letter in response to a story about a critic of a program designed to make schools inclusive and safe for students of all sexual orientations and gender identities. She explained what school can be like for LGBTQIA2S+ kids and why the program is important. "I believe the new curriculum… will help break down barriers and encourage discussion and understanding," she wrote. The editor of the paper said Anna's letter was "concise, passionate and eloquent."

GET A PAPER ROUTE

When my eldest daughter was eight, she followed in my foot-steps and got a paper route. Every week, she delivers the local paper to dozens of our neighbors. It's been a great way to meet people in our community, get exercise and earn money. My daughter is proud to play a critical role in ensuring that her neighbors know what's happening in the community. She also likes leafing through the grocery-store flyers to see what treats are on sale so she can try to convince me to buy them!

BECOME A JOURNALIST

One of the best ways you can make a difference in the media industry is by becoming a journalist. And you're never too young to get started.

Start Practicing

A great way to begin working on the skills you need is to walk around your neighborhood with a pencil and notebook and look for things happening. Maybe you'll see people speeding through a school zone, or perhaps you'll witness a cat killing a bird. You can then ask your friends, family members and neighbors what they think about the issues and events you've observed and write stories based on what you saw, heard and learned.

You can even use your screen time to hone your jour-nalism skills by playing BBC iReporter, an exciting game in which you become a journalist covering breaking news.

Take a Class

You may be able to find classes or camps in your commu-nity where you can learn journalism skills. A good place to

EXTRA! EXTRA!

Lots of famous people were newspaper carriers when they were kids, including US President Joe Biden, civil rights leader Martin Luther King, Jr., Disney founder Walt Disney and hockey star Wayne Gretzky. The Newspaper Carrier Hall of Fame honors carriers who have gone on to do great things in their lives, and International Newspaper Carrier Day celebrates all carriers every October.

NAYEEM KALAM/GETTY IMAGES

look for these opportunities is at colleges and universities that have journalism programs. You can also look for online workshops offered by journalism organizations. The Canadian Youth Journalism Project, for instance, offers free online workshops on topics like investigative journalism and making media more inclusive.

Join the School Paper

If you're lucky, your school will have a student newspaper or a journalism class. However, both are much more common in high schools than in elementary and middle schools. I still remember my high-school journalism class and writing about the student-council election and the increasing cost of slushies—both very important issues!

Become a Correspondent

Once you get some experience, you can apply to be a kid correspondent with a media outlet that has them or ask your local media outlets if they'd be interested in taking on a cub reporter.

START A NEWS OUTLET

Once you know how to put together news stories, you can start your own news outlet. It may sound daunting, but lots of kids have done it, often with the help of some friends or their parents. You and your fellow journalists could make a newspaper by writing and editing stories, taking photos, making graphics and creating a layout with a free app. You could then print your paper and deliver it to people in your neighborhood or school, or send it out

via email. You could also make a news website by purchasing a domain name and using a template to do the layout. You could even try to get a grant or get some local businesses to advertise in your publication in order to cover your costs.

SUPPORT YOUR MEDIA

Media outlets and organizations that help journalists often need support. You can help them by becoming a member, subscriber or volunteer. You could also hold a fundraiser like a bottle drive, bake sale or car wash and donate the proceeds. If your fundraiser is interesting enough (say, a dunk tank with the mayor of your city), you may even get media attention!

Journalism plays a vital role in our daily lives, and you can help ensure that it continues to do so by getting involved and speaking up. Your voice matters, and the more kids who get involved in journalism today, the better the news will be in the future.

During the pandemic, San Francisco journalist and parent Chris Colin created a newspaper by and for kids called *Six Feet of Separation*. CHRIS COLIN

TORY MCNALLY

STAR REPORTER:
HATTY HAWTHORNE

Like most kids, eight-year-old Hatty Hawthorne was getting pretty bored when schools first closed during the COVID-19 pandemic in 2020. So she decided to start a newspaper for her Winnipeg neighbors called *Hatty's News*. She delivered it on her scooter to about 40 subscribers, who paid 50 cents an issue, helping her save up to buy a Polaroid camera.

Hatty's News included jokes, crafts, recipes, contests, interviews, investigations and an advice column. One of her investigations started after she saw Chinese food being delivered to the local elementary school. "Do the custodians live at Queenston School? Investigation to follow," she wrote.

Hatty's advice column was particularly popular. One letter from a "dog-less dog lover" asked what they should do now that physical-distancing rules prevented them from petting other people's dogs. Hatty advised them to get a robotic dog or borrow a dog for the weekend through the Winnipeg Humane Society's staycation program. Solid advice!

"I think it is important for kids to get involved in the news because if kids don't get involved, it will not last to the next generation. It is important for kids to know what is happening in the world." —Hatty Hawthorne

Glossary

abolitionist—a person who favors ending a practice, such as slavery

artificial intelligence (AI)—the ability of a computer program or a machine to perform tasks that normally require human intelligence, such as decision-making

business model—a system for doing business, including products and/or services, revenue sources and customers

byline—a line in a newspaper, magazine or online news story naming the author of the article

circulation—the number of copies of a newspaper or magazine that are sold and/or distributed

conflicts of interest—situations in which people are in a position to derive personal benefit from actions taken or decisions made in their official capacity

context—the circumstances surrounding an event, statement or idea that ensure it can be fully understood and assessed

crowdfund—fund a project or venture by raising money from a large number of people who each contribute a relatively small amount

cub reporter—a young or inexperienced reporter

data—facts and/or statistics collected for reference and/or analysis

democracy—a system of government in which people have a say in how it is run by voting for leaders

exposé—a news story that reveals something that was previously unknown

impartial—treating all sides of arguments equally

marginalized—to be put in a position of little or no importance, influence or power within a society or group

media conglomerates—companies that own multiple media businesses

misogyny—hatred of or prejudice against women

monopoly—a company's or group's exclusive possession or control over a good or service

newsworthy—considered interesting enough to the public or a specific audience to be reported on

ochre—an earthy pigment that's usually red or yellow

paywalls—systems that prevent a person from accessing a website without being a paid subscriber

pen name—a fake name used by a writer to protect or conceal their true identity

petroglyphs—carvings or inscriptions, often prehistoric, on rock surfaces

pictographs—drawings or paintings, often prehistoric, on rock surfaces

political spectrum—the range of political opinions that exist from the progressive left wing to the conservative right wing

post-traumatic stress disorder—a mental health condition that's triggered by a terrifying event

public money—money that has been collected by governments, usually through taxes

rations—specific amounts of goods allowed to individuals, especially in times of shortages, such as during wars

scribes—people who copy documents by hand

shareholders—people who own shares in a company

solidarity—unity among people who have a common interest or objective

spokespersons—people who speak on behalf of organizations

steam engine—an engine that uses steam to generate power and perform mechanical work

tax havens—countries or other places with low or no corporate tax where non-residents can set up businesses to avoid paying higher taxes in their regions

trolls—people who make deliberately offensive or provocative comments or posts online

undocumented migrants—people who live in a country without legal authorization to be or remain there

Universal Declaration of Human Rights—an international document adopted by the United Nations that guarantees the rights and freedoms of all people

whistleblower—a person who informs an individual or an organization of another person's or organization's unlawful or immoral activity

Resources

PRINT

Bohrer, Jessica and Sandy. *Your Voice Is Your Superpower! A Beginner's Guide to Freedom of Speech (and the First Amendment).* City Point Press Kids, 2020.

Copeland, Cynthia L. *Cub.* Algonquin Books, 2020.

Crysdale, Joy. *Fearless Female Journalists.* Second Story Press, 2010.

Dakers, Diane. *Information Literacy and Fake News.* Crabtree Publishing Company, 2018.

Grant, Joyce. *Can You Believe It? How to Spot Fake News and Find the Facts.* Kids Can Press, 2022.

Mahoney, Ellen. *Nellie Bly and Investigative Journalism for Kids: Mighty Muckrakers from the Golden Age to Today.* Chicago Review Press, 2015.

ONLINE

Canadian Journalism Foundation: cjf-fjc.ca

Canadian Youth Journalism Project: canadianyouthjournalismproject.com

Columbia Journalism Review: cjr.org

Committee to Protect Journalists: cpj.org

Freedom of the Press Foundation: freedom.press

International Consortium of Investigative Journalists: icij.org

Journalists for Human Rights: jhr.ca

J-Source (the Canadian Journalism Project): j-source.ca

MediaWise Teen Fact-Checking Network: poynter.org/teen-fact-checking-network

NewseumED: newseumed.org

Poynter Institute: poynter.org

Reporters Without Borders: rsf.org

Reuters Institute: reutersinstitute.politics.ox.ac.uk

Student Press Freedom Day: studentpressfreedom.org

Student Press Law Center: splc.org

Teaching Kids News: teachingkidsnews.com

NEWS SOURCES FOR KIDS

CBC Kids News: cbc.ca/kidsnews

Chirp, Chickadee and *Owl* magazines: owlkids.com

CNN 10: cnn.com/cnn10

KidNuz: kidnuz.org

KidsPost: washingtonpost.com/lifestyle/kidspost

National Geographic Kids: kids.nationalgeographic.com

NBC Nightly News with Lester Holt: Kids Edition: nbcnews.com/nightlykids

News for Kids: NewsForKids.net

Teen Kids News: teenkidsnews.com

The Ten News: thetennews.com

Time for Kids: timeforkids.com

Science News Explores: snexplores.org

YR Media: yr.media

ONLINE NEWS GAMES AND QUIZZES

Bad News: getbadnews.com

BBC iReporter: bbc.co.uk/ireporter

Doubt It?: doubtit.ca

Factitious: factitious-pandemic.augamestudio.com

Fake or Foto: fakeorfoto.autodesk.com

Fake Out: newsliteracy.ca/fakeOut

Go Viral!: goviralgame.com

Reality Check: mediasmarts.ca/sites/mediasmarts/files/games/reality-check

Spot the Troll: spotthetroll.org

FILM

Raise Your Voice: raiseyourvoicedocumentary.com

The Social Dilemma: thesocialdilemma.com

Acknowledgments

Giving credit where credit is due is critical in journalism, so here we go!

I was very fortunate to have some incredible journalism teachers over the years: Nicolas Rebselj at Earl Marriott Secondary School, who sparked my interest in the industry; Don Gibb at Toronto Metropolitan University, who shared many tips on how to be an ace reporter, including to always ask for the names of animals involved in news stories (because who doesn't love hearing about a swan named Bae who was rescued by a cyclist in New York City and got to ride the subway to safety?); and David Hayes at Toronto Metropolitan University, who inspired me to go deeper with my reporting and writing to help people truly connect with stories. I've also had the great pleasure of working with and learning from dozens of talented and caring journalists—from interns to editors in chief—far too many to name here. Thanks to all of you.

I'm also incredibly grateful to all the journalists and researchers who produced the work featured on these pages and those who took time out of their busy schedules to speak with me for this book. Thank you for sharing your expertise and experience and for the important work you do to keep people informed about the news and the news business.

This book was a big team project, just like putting together a newspaper. Thanks to the entire team at Orca: editor Kirstie Hudson, a former journalist who offered expert insight and input; illustrator Julie McLaughlin, who brought this book to life with her art and is responsible for my favorite part of it (the illustration of the raccoon in the vending machine on page 4); designer Troy Cunningham, who put these pages together beautifully; and all the people behind the scenes.

My family is an ongoing source of support and laughter. Hugs and high-fives to my children, Ocea and Elodie, for listening to early versions of this book and telling me what was interesting and what was boring. (I cut most of the boring stuff!) And thank you to my husband, Gabe, for acting as my personal research assistant and copyeditor.

I was absolutely thrilled to receive a BC Arts Council grant to write this book. (You should have seen my happy dance!) Thank you to the council and the Province of British Columbia for supporting this project.

Finally, thank you to all the journalists who are working hard under tremendous pressure in an ever-changing environment, especially the young ones who are entering the industry with fresh ideas and optimism. You and your work are invaluable.

Index

Page numbers in **bold** indicate an image caption.

TAYLOR ROADES/THE NARWHAL

RAINA DELISLE is an award-winning writer whose work has been featured in *Today's Parent*, *Chatelaine*, CBC and the *Globe and Mail*, among many other publications. She has worked in journalism and government communications, giving her a unique perspective on the media industry. Her first book, *Fashion Forward: Striving for Sustainable Style*, was published in 2022. Raina lives in Victoria, British Columbia.

MELANIE GRISAK

JULIE MCLAUGHLIN is an award-winning illustrator of numerous children's books, including *Pride Puppy!*, *Little Cloud* and *Why We Live Where We Live*, winner of the 2015 Norma Fleck Award for Canadian Children's Non-Fiction. Her work with various editorial, advertising and publishing clients can be seen around the world. Julie grew up on the Prairies and now resides on Vancouver Island, British Columbia.